The Children of
MICRONESIA

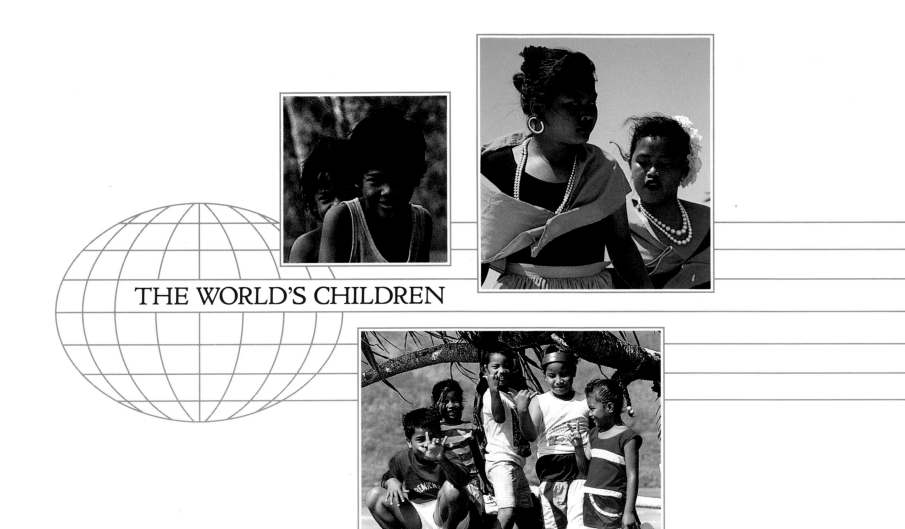

THE WORLD'S CHILDREN

The Children of
MICRONESIA

JULES HERMES

Carolrhoda Books, Inc./Minneapolis

For Steve

Text and photographs copyright © 1994 by Jules Hermes
Illustration copyright © 1994 by Carolrhoda Books, Inc.

Carolrhoda Books Inc. c/o The Lerner Group
241 First Avenue North, Minneapolis, MN 55401

LIBRARY OF CONGRESS CATALOGING-IN-PUBLICATION DATA

Hermes, Jules M., 1962-
   The children of Micronesia / by Jules Hermes
     p. cm. — (The World's children)
   ISBN 0-87614-819-4
   1. Micronesia—Social life and customs—Juvenile
literature. 2. Children—Micronesia—Social life and
customs. [1. Micronesia—Social life and customs.] I.
Title. II. Series: World's children (Minneapolis, Minn.)
DU500.H47 1994
996.5—dc20   93-31268
                                                         CIP
                                                          AC

Manufactured in the United States of America

1 2 3 4 5 6 – I/JR – 99 98 97 96 95 94

Author's Note:

When I first decided to go to Micronesia, I soon discovered that most Americans know little or nothing of this vast region in the Pacific. Micronesia's history is complicated because so many countries have colonized these islands over the course of hundreds of years, and the islands have been wrapped in secrecy due to their importance as military bases in World Wars I and II. Until 1978, most of Micronesia was part of the Trust Territory of the Pacific Islands, awarded to the United States after the defeat of Japan in World War II. The Trust Territory included the Federated States of Micronesia (made up of Kosrae, Pohnpei, Yap, and Truk), the Northern Marianas, the Marshall Islands, and the Republic of Palau. In 1982, however, the Federated States of Micronesia signed the Compact of Free Association with the United States, the Northern Marianas became a commonwealth, the Marshall Islands remained a trust territory, and the Republic of Palau remained undecided as to their relationship to the United States.

The combination of colonization and foreign influence has altered the values and customs of the Micronesian people, especially the children. Where learning to navigate canoes by the stars was once a vital part of every young boy's education, they now learn to drive cars. Girls used to stay home with their mothers, learning to weave, farm, and take care of the household. Today they study history, science, and go on to college. For many Micronesians, this signals the beginning of the decline of their culture. For others, it means greater opportunity for the future. And while Micronesia is still considered a poor region because of its dependence on aid from the United States, it is virtually free of poverty, homelessness, and crime. It is a place where the youth still respect the older generations, and where extended families live and work together. Here, one may discover secrets of wars past, people who have held onto their traditions, and children who believe their islands are a gift from God and call them paradise.

Above: *An outrigger sailboat on Becheyal Beach on Yap Island.* Left: *Managaha Island off the coast of Saipan in the Northern Mariana Islands*

Thousands of years ago, people from Southeast Asia left their homes, travelling by outrigger sailboats and rafts, and came to a place in the Pacific Ocean known today as Micronesia, which means "small islands." Scattered throughout the Pacific Ocean between Hawaii and the Philippines, the thousands of small islands that make up Micronesia stretch across an area more than one thousand miles long and two thousand miles wide. The combined land mass of these islands, however, equals only that of the state of Rhode Island.

Perhaps the first people who came to Micronesia were fleeing from some tragedy in their homeland, or maybe they were blown off course. For whatever reasons these people came to Micronesia, they probably found pristine islands, clean water, and a sort of isolation that sheltered them from the rest of the world.

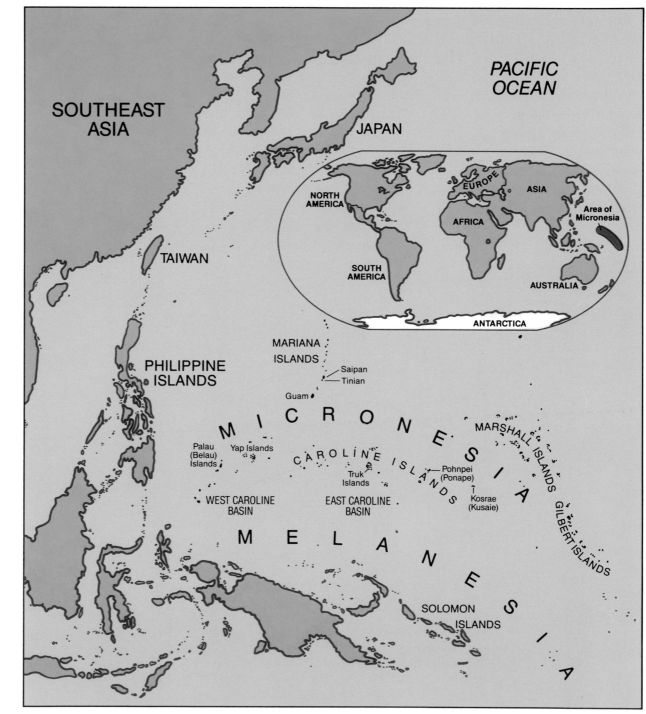

Ancient records indicate that early settlers on the islands of Micronesia often fought with each other and with the ruling *saudeleurs,* or native kings, who they believed had great powers and supernatural strength. The *saudeleurs* ruled from a place called Nan Madol on the island of Pohnpei (also known as Ponape). Nan Madol, which means "places in between," consisted of 92 human-made small islands, or islets, constructed over a period of 200 to 300 years. Each islet, crisscrossed by waterways, was used for a special purpose. The women's quarters were on a separate islet, while other islets served as places to perform religious sacrifices and burials. The rest of the islanders lived quite differently from the *saudeleurs.* Most lived in huts made of materials found on the island with members of their clan, or family. They grew their own food, caught fish, and navigated the waterways.

Right: *Wall mural from Pohnpei. From as early as A.D. 1100,* saudeleurs *ruled Pohnpei from Nan Madol, a grouping of stone and basalt compounds that are believed to have been a religious center. Legend says it was founded by two brothers named Olsohpa and Olsihpa, wise and holy men who sailed to Pohnpei from Katau Peidi to the west. They used magic to make the stones fly into place on Temwen Island, where the stones remain today.*

Today Pohnpei remains the lush volcanic island that attracted the *saudeleurs* so many years ago. About 30,000 people live on Pohnpei and the nine tiny outer islands that surround it.

Above: *Pingalap Island, one of Pohnpei's nine outer islands.* Right: *The beautiful waterfalls and rivers of Pohnpei's lush interior are vital to the lives of the Pohnpeians.*

Yorra lives near Nan Madol on the island of Pohnpei. Yorra's grandfather is the *nahnmwarki,* or traditional chief, of Net district on Pohnpei. King Isokele-kel established the dynasty of *nahnmwarkis* in A.D. 1628 by overthrowing the *saudeleurs* at Nan Madol with 333 soldiers. *Nahnmwarkis,* along with their seconds-in-command, called *nahnkens,* are highly regarded and still control the five districts of Pohnpei. Many Pohnpeians believe an ancestral spirit guides the island chiefs.

Yorra

Nan Madol

None of the traditional chiefs, however, controls the modern city of Kolonia, Pohnpei's business center. And while Yorra's family's status makes her one of the royalty of Pohnpei, growing up on Pohnpei is not so different from growing up in the United States. She watches television, drinks Coca-Cola, and asks her mom for her allowance in U.S. dollars, which is the currency used on Pohnpei.

Yorra attends the many feasts that mark special occasions on Pohnpei, such as when titles are handed down to members of the nobility class. Pohnpeians belong to one of three social classes. The royalty are those with direct bloodlines to the chief, such as a daughter, son, sister, or brother. The nobility are those relatives less closely related to the *nahnmwarki,* such as a nephew, niece, or cousin. Commoners are those who have little or no family ties to the *nahnmwarki.*

Above: *Yorra and her friends.*
Left: *Men and women bring* sakau, taro, *and breadfruit for a feast.*

Right: *Pigs prepared for a feast.*
Below: *The* nahs *of Net district*

Men and women of all classes bring Yorra's grandfather, the *nahnmwarki,* breadfruit, *taro,* pigs, and *sakau* from their farms. They slaughter pigs for the feast, and pound *sakau,* a traditional drink made from the root of the pepper plant, for members of the royalty and nobility inside the *nahs*—the ceremonial meetinghouse of the district. Pohnpeians consider many pigs and *sakau* plants a sign of wealth. Some feasts can last for as long as four or five days. Funerals, for example, can continue for days, depending on whose death is being mourned. Other ceremonies, such as weddings, usually last an entire day.

Left: *Dionne*. Below: *A typhoon destroyed Dionne's neighbor's house. Even though it was built of concrete, the typhoon ripped it apart.*

Not long ago, a typhoon hit Pohnpei. Dionne, one of Yorra's best friends, lives in a house made of concrete, unlike most Pohnpeian homes, which are built of wood and tin. Dionne's neighbor's house was torn apart during the typhoon, but Dionne's home was left untouched. Typhoons are a major danger in the Micronesian islands, though some islands are more susceptible than others. Usually, concrete homes can withstand the strong winds and rain brought by the typhoons. But sometimes typhoons are so strong that they wipe out an entire district, including the concrete buildings.

From the top of Sokehs Rock, the highest point of Sokehs district, Dionne can see much of her island and the narrow landing strip of Pohnpei's airport.

15

Maxon rides a water buffalo

A lush rain forest covers Pohnpei's interior and is one of the wettest spots on earth. Only one village, Salapwuk, is located in the interior. Four-year-old Maxon lives in Salapwuk with his family. Accessible only by a footpath, Salapwuk was the first village on Pohnpei. Here in the village, life remains much the same as it has been for hundreds of years.

As his father did before him, Maxon's father grows the family's food on his plot of land. The family catches fish from the nearby river, and at night Maxon's father will make *sakau*, the traditional drink. Maxon goes to a small village school during the day. After school he likes to play in the river or ride on the water buffalo.

Above: *To make the* sakau *drink, the* sakau *plant is pounded to a pulp, squeezed through hibiscus leaves, and served in half a coconut shell. Some people believe they must keep their eyes closed while drinking from the cup to avoid any spell that may have been cast upon the cup.* Right: *Temperatures remain hot and humid year-round. Children keep cool by playing in the rivers that run through Pohnpei's interior.*

The Yapese of Yap Island live even more traditional lives than the islanders of Pohnpei. The Yapese were considered the greatest voyagers of the western Pacific. The outer islanders, the people who come from the smaller islands off the coast of Yap Island, are highly skilled traditional navigators of the seas.

Calvin steers his raft.

Left: *The stone path to the Weloy* peebai. Below: *Stone money rests outside a district meetinghouse. Basalt stones were quarried from the islands of Palau hundreds of years ago by Yap's first inhabitants. The people shaped the stones into a circle with a hole in the center and brought them back to Yap. Clans used the stone money for barter and trade. Even today, the stone money is not allowed to be removed from Yap.*

Boys like Calvin still ply the narrow waterways by raft. Calvin comes from the Weloy district. A stone path near his home leads to the traditional meetinghouse called a *peebai*. The *peebai* serves as a meeting place for the community and as the site of the bank of stone money. Like gold in the western world, stone money set the standard for money in Yapese society long ago. The value of the heavy, round stones, which sit outside the *peebai*, was not determined by their size, but by the difficulty of their journey hundreds of years ago by raft from the island of Palau about 600 miles away. Although the United States dollar is taking its place, stone money still holds its value in Yapese society and can be used in Yap for important purchases.

Carefully tended gardens and farmland distinguish the beautiful villages of Yap. Most Yapese grow a great variety of fruits and vegetables to feed their families. Palm trees, coconut trees, and exotic flowers, like the bird-of-paradise, grow wild in the jungle.

Giltamag comes from Maap district, located on Yap's eastern coast. Giltamag likes to visit his uncle Yanmog, who grows tall stalks of sugarcane as well as papayas, oranges, and bananas in his garden. They often go spearfishing at night after everyone else has gone to bed.

Above: *Giltamag's mother has a small shop in Colonia, a village located at the center of Yap Island, where she sells canned foods, coconuts, and cold drinks. Built on stilts, the shop rests over the water. Opposite page, left: A bird-of-paradise flower. Opposite page, right: Giltamag wears the traditional* thu *around his waist.*

The languages and customs of the smaller, outer islands of Yap differ greatly from those on the main island. Many people from the main island cannot communicate with people from the outer islands because their languages are so different.

Siren comes from an outer island and can speak English as well as the language of her island. Siren prefers the way of life on the outer islands, where there are no cars and no electricity. Boys still learn the ancient secrets of navigating their outrigger sailboats by watching and learning patterns of the waves and stars. They say they can navigate by the stars even during the day. Siren says the men and boys who study this ancient navigation would never reveal their secrets to an outsider.

Most of all, the Yapese value the teaching of their traditional ways to their children. Retaining their heritage has become more important here than on any other Micronesian island.

Below: Siren is dressed in a traditional dance costume.

People on the more remote Carolinian islands still practice some of the ancient customs, such as tattooing. Sometimes men and women tattoo their entire bodies. Some men pierce their noses by placing a bone in a hole between the nostrils. Here, a group of young boys watches a man get a tattoo.

Most Yapese adults carry a handwoven betel-nut basket. The baskets hold aged and hollowed coconuts filled with lime powder, betel nuts, and leaves. They split open the nut and sprinkle it with the lime powder, which is made from crushed coral. Then they wrap it in a pepper leaf and chew the entire bundle whole. The betel nut releases a red juice that stains teeth and gums. Betel nut chewers claim this makes their teeth cavity-proof.

23

Left: *Yap Lagoon*. Below left: *Tony and Patrick*. Below right: *A faluw*

Yapese boys perform the warrior stick dance, one of the traditions taught to them by the men of their village at the faluw.

By night, Yap Lagoon reflects the orange setting sun. Waterways from the lagoon lead to the village of Gilman, where Tony and Patrick live. After school the boys often go into the jungle and hunt for birds. Most likely, however, they will only shoot down betel nuts.

On their way home, Patrick and Tony walk past the old men's house of Gilman, called a *faluw. Faluws* once served as schools where boys came to learn from the elder men of their villages. Women were for-bidden to enter *faluws.* Now most boys and girls of Yap Island go to a government school and learn math, science, and other subjects—all taught in English. Some children still go to the *faluw* to learn about Yapese traditions.

Above left: *Mutti.* Above right: *Bert's mother, Sepe, makes the traditional* mar-mar, *which is worn by many Carolinians.* Left: *Sleeping Lady mountain*

Mutti comes from the island of Kosrae (also known as Kusaie), the Carolinian island closest to Hawaii. She lives in a quiet bay with her aunts, uncles, and cousins. From the boat docks near her home, Mutti can see Sleeping Lady, the mountain in Kosrae's lush interior that resembles a woman lying on her back. Compared to the other Micronesian islands, Kosrae has seen very little development. Most Kosraens are farmers and live along the coast of the island, where they can grow most of the food they need.

Bert and his family live next door to Mutti. Bert and his sister, Honda, hike around Lela Island, located at the center of Kosrae. On Sundays the adults observe strict quiet and rest, so the children entertain themselves by searching for the buried treasure of the notorious American whaler, Bully Hayes. Bert says Bully's ship, the *Leonora*, sank off the shores of Kosrae in the 1800s and remains undiscovered. Bert hopes that one day he will find the gold and treasure hidden on Bully's sunken ship, and if he does find it, he plans to share his wealth with his family.

Bert, his brother, and his friends give the "everything's fine" sign in Kosraen.

William lives on the other side of Kosrae, in Utwe. During the day, William and his parents wade into the bay to catch fish with a huge net. At night, William and his father sail their boat farther out into the ocean to catch flying fish. With a 15-foot bamboo pole and a net attached, William and his father scoop fish out of the air. A lantern placed near the water attracts the fish to the surface. The fish can fly 10 feet out of the water. On a good night, William and his father bring in around 100 fish.

Left: *William.* Below: *Kosraens fishing in the bay at Utwe*

Kosraens eat plenty of fish, pig, and squid. William likes to prepare pig and squid on the *uhmw*, which is a mound of heated rocks where the food is cooked. His father skins and cleans a pig, and his mother washes some squid. Then they heat the rocks of the *uhmw* and place the food on the red-hot rocks. They cover the *uhmw* with banana leaves and leave the food to cook on the rocks for several hours.

Above: *The* uhmw. Left: *Typical food for the* uhmw

29

Melinda lives on the island of Saipan, which is part of the Northern Mariana Islands. Saipan was called "Island of Thieves" by explorer Ferdinand Magellan, the first European explorer to arrive on the island in the 1500s. For centuries, whalers and trade ships stopped on Saipan when travelling between the Americas and Asia. Melinda is a Chamorro, a native of the Mariana Islands. She speaks the Chamorro language as well as English. In the 1600s, missionaries came to the Northern Marianas, teaching the English language and converting the Chamorros to Christianity. Although Melinda is Christian, she, like many Chamorros, also believes in the ancient religion of her people. They worship their ancestors' spirits and will often consult a medicine man instead of a medical doctor to cure them of sickness and disease.

Right: *On Good Friday before Easter Sunday, Melinda joins thousands of people in a procession to the top of Mount Tagpochau. The worshipers carry a large wooden cross up the mountain and place it on the summit.*
Below: *A view of Saipan from Mount Tagpochau*

Every year since Melinda was two years old, she has joined her family in the Easter procession to Saipan's highest peak, Mount Tagpochau. From here she can see the entire island of Saipan and the deep waters of the Mariana Trench. More than 36,000 feet deep, the trench is among the deepest waters on Earth. Melinda can also see Forbidden Island, which is believed by most children to be stalked at night by the ghosts of their ancestors. From Mount Tagpochau she can also see the neighboring island of Tinian, where the American bomber jet, *Enola Gay,* took off for the flight to Hiroshima and Nagasaki during World War II and dropped the only atomic bombs ever used in war.

Saipan has been involved in many wars, none of which have been their own. Countries fought each other for control of Saipan because of its central location in the Pacific Ocean. During World War II, the United States launched an attack on Japan from the Northern Mariana Islands. The islands were used as military bases for refueling ships, storing military equipment, and launching attacks.

Above: *Frankie sits between his friends.*
Right: *Every Sunday Frankie helps serve mass with two of his closest friends. This service, held in the jungle, celebrates the feast day of Our Lady of Lourdes.*

Left: *A U.S. merchant marine ship and a local fishing boat in Saipan's lagoon.* Below: *A Japanese tank from World War II*

Frankie lives on Saipan, and he and his friends like to go "boonie stomping," or hiking around the island, which is littered with relics of World War II. On the weekends, Frankie likes to go to Managaha Island. During the half-hour boat ride to Managaha Island, Frankie can see the massive merchant marine ships in the bay. He says that the tanks and military equipment on the ship were used in the Persian Gulf War in 1990. Saipan is one of only three places in the world where these ships are anchored.

As a result of the continuous foreign occupation and warfare on these islands, many Chamorros have lost respect and trust for foreigners and are very protective of their culture and the islands.

Mona wins the title "Miss Mariana High School Queen."

The Mariana Islands north of Saipan are mostly uninhabited. Some have active volcanoes on them, while others are simply too small for people to live on. Mona Taisacan's mother was born on a northern island called Anatahan. Volcanic eruptions formed the beautiful rivers and beaches of black sand there. Typhoons and a lack of drinking water and food forced the small number of people on Anatahan to be evacuated when Mona was just a baby, and now she and her family live on Saipan. Mona's mother worries that her daughter will not learn the traditions of her island, as the larger islands like Saipan and Guam become more and more influenced by

the United States and Japan. Foreigners pay millions of dollars to lease large areas of the islands and build hotels and resorts. This brings more money and a higher standard of living to the Micronesians, but it also means that they may no longer live and work on the land in the way that they have for generations.

Above: *Some islands face serious water pollution problems, because garbage is burned in open areas next to the ocean. Dumps like this one on Saipan cause problems for the marine life as well.* Right: *A new car in front of a corrugated tin house is a common sight on the islands. People use cars for transportation even on islands only three miles long.*

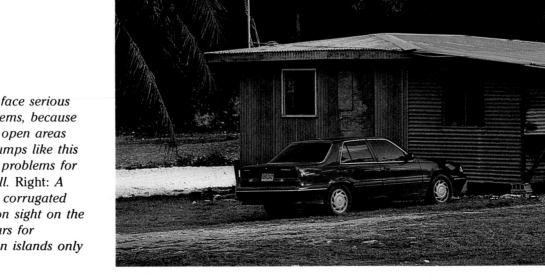

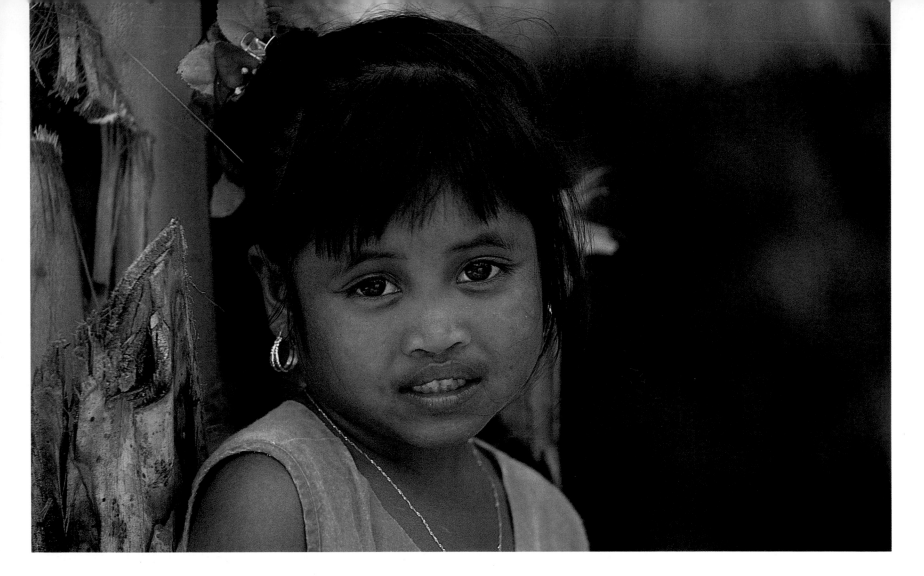

Leela

Like Saipan, the modern city of Koror on the island of Palau (also known as Belau) has enormous resort hotels. Tourists stroll through the beautiful city parks, where teenagers play in organized basketball tournaments.

Even in this modern-looking city, traditions remain. Leela, a four-year-old from Koror, attends a very traditional Palauan event. To celebrate Leela's aunt's upcoming marriage, the bride's family holds a "coming out" ceremony. After a series of hot herbal baths, Leela's aunt appears before relatives and friends covered in oil and a ground herb called turmeric. Hot bath ceremonies signify both a birth and a marriage. Leela, like all Palauan women, will also have a hot bath ceremony and a "coming out" celebration when she grows up and marries.

Left: *Teenagers in Koror play European and American sports such as basketball.*
Below: *During a "coming out" ceremony, relatives and friends dance around the woman, giving her one-dollar bills and covering her with herbs and warm water.*

Jeanette will also have a "coming out" celebration when she gets married, even though her father is American. Jeanette's father, Jerry, came to Micronesia from the United States more than 25 years ago. When the United States was awarded trust of the Micronesian Islands after World War II, many Americans came to fill government positions and to work in the Peace Corps. Some Americans married Micronesians and settled down on the islands. Jerry married Irene, a woman from Palau. They have three children, and although the children follow many of their father's American ways, they also participate in their mother's Palauan customs.

Palau has a matrilineal society, which means that Palauans trace their family lines by their mothers' relatives, rather than by their fathers' relatives. Women control the land, wealth, and all decision making, as well as the daily chores.

Above: *Jeanette and her family.* Left: *Jeanette takes communion for the first time.* Opposite page: *Jeanette's mother has taught her children about the important Palauan legends that are carved on storyboards, such as the one pictured here. Introduced to the Palauans by the Japanese, storyboards retell Palauan legends that were once passed down only by storytelling.*

In Palauan society, a family is considered very wealthy if they have all female children, while a family with many boys is considered poor. Female family members hold "house raising parties" where females contribute hundreds or thousands of dollars so that their brother can build his home. Jeanette, along with her American father and her Palauan mother, participates in house raising parties and other Palauan celebrations.

Stephania Rios and her friends perform the lambada.

Opposite page, left and right: *Throughout Micronesia one can see relics of the Spaniards. A Catholic church and cemetery near Stephania's home reveal Spanish influences. More than half of all Micronesians follow the Catholic faith, which was introduced by the Spanish.* Opposite page, below: *Japanese prayer sticks found on Saipan were placed on the island in memory of the Japanese who lost their lives there.*

People from other countries have influenced the lives of Micronesians for centuries. This influence from the outside world began in the 1500s, when the Portuguese and the Spanish first landed on the islands. When the Germans, British, Japanese, Americans, and Australians followed, each country left a lasting mark on the culture of the islands.

Stephania Rios lives on Saipan. Her grandfather was Japanese and her grandmother was German. A Spanish family named Rios adopted her Japanese grandfather after his parents were killed in World War II. The Spanish had control of the Northern Mariana Islands until 1899, when they sold the islands to Germany after they lost the Spanish-American War. Stephania's grandfather took his adoptive family's Spanish last name, as well as some of their Spanish traditions. Stephania learned to dance the Spanish *lambada* from her Spanish teacher.

The most recent immigrants to Micronesia are Koreans. Lee's parents came from Korea 10 years ago looking for work. Lee's mother works as a maid and her father works on the roads. Although the family is more than one thousand miles from their homeland, they have retained their cultural identity and traditions through festivals and ceremonies in their Korean community.

Kim and Lee wear ceremonial wedding costumes from their homeland, Korea.

Right: *Korean youths in Micronesia perform traditional Korean music.* Below: *Chinese workers are taken by bus to garment factories, where they often work 18 hours a day and are paid about two dollars an hour.*

Most of the Chinese people who have come to Micronesia in search of jobs have had to work in garment factories, where working conditions are poor, the hours are long, and the pay is low. In spite of these hardships, most feel fortunate to have work outside of China, because in Micronesia they can earn enough money to send some home to their families in China.

The mix of old and new can be seen throughout the islands.

The increasing presence of Japanese and American culture in Micronesia is changing life on the islands, just as other nations have had an impact in the past. And, as they have done for the last several centuries, the people continue to hold onto their traditions as they also adopt new ways of life. Micronesians are often forced to choose between development and tradition, and development usually wins. Some feel it is up to the youth to maintain the Micronesians' way of life in the Pacific. Some feel it is time to change and accept the ways of the modern world. Modern life, as we call it, has found these islanders again and again, and the beauty and solitude of the islands is in danger of disappearing forever. But, Micronesians continue to learn to live with changes, just as they have learned to live with the ever-changing tide.

Young Micronesian dancers perform a traditional Carolinian dance during a cultural festival.

Pronunciation Note:

Most of the foreign words used in this book come from the variety of languages spoken in Micronesia. Many of these languages were first written into the English alphabet just 150 years ago. Some spellings and pronunciations of words are still changing, but, in general, you can figure out how to pronounce each word simply by sounding it out. Please note, however, that "i" is usually pronounced "ee" and "w" is silent. For example, *nahnmwarki* is pronounced nahn-mar-kee.

Glossary

faluw: a traditional men's meeting house
mar-mar: a garland of flowers worn on the head
nahnken: the second-in-command of a district on Pohnpei
nahnmwarki: the traditional leader of a district on Pohnpei
nahs: a ceremonial meeting house of a district on Pohnpei
peebai: a traditional meeting house on Yap
sakau: a drink made from the root of a pepper plant
saudeleurs: native kings who ruled on Pohnpei more than 800 years ago
thu: an article of clothing worn on Yap
uhmw: an oven made of heated rocks, sometimes placed in a pit underground

Index